MW00785653

Scratch Pegasus

Also by Stephen Kessler

POETRY

Burning Daylight 2007
Tell It to the Rabbis 2001
After Modigliani 2000
Living Expenses 1980
Beauty Fatigue 1978
Thirteen Ways of Deranging an Angel 1977
Poem to Walt Disney 1976
Nostalgia of the Fortuneteller 1975

TRANSLATION

Poems of Consummation (poems by Vicente Aleixandre) 2013
Desolation of the Chimera (poems by Luis Cernuda) 2009
Eyeseas (poems by Raymond Queneau, translated with Daniela Hurezanu) 2008
Written in Water (prose poems by Luis Cernuda) 2004
Aphorisms (prose by César Vallejo) 2002
Heights of Machu Picchu (poem by Pablo Neruda) 2001
Ode to Typography (poem by Pablo Neruda) 1998
Save Twilight (poems by Julio Cortázar) 1997
From Beirut (poem by Mahmoud Darwish) 1992
Akrílica (poems by Juan Felipe Herrera, translated with Sesshu Foster) 1989
The Funhouse (novel by Fernando Alegría) 1986
Changing Centuries (poems by Fernando Alegría) 1985
Widows (novel by Ariel Dorfman) 1983
Homage to Neruda (poems by eight Chilean poets) 1978
Destruction or Love (poems by Vicente Aleixandre) 1976

PROSE

The Tolstoy of the Zulus: On Culture, Arts & Letters (essays) 2011
The Mental Traveler (novel) 2009
Moving Targets: On Poets, Poetry & Translation (essays) 2008

EDITOR

The Sonnets by Jorge Luis Borges 2010

Scratch Pegasus

Stephen Kessler

Swan Scythe Press

Acknowledgment is due to the editors of the following periodicals where some of these poems first appeared: *Calibanonline, The Cincinnati Review, Clade Song, Coe Review, 48th Street Press Broadside Series, Gargoyle, Ginosko, Mission at Tenth, New American Writing, Or, Osiris, Parthenon West Review, Perihelion, Pinyon, Red Wheelbarrow, The Redwood Coast Review, Santa Cruz Weekly,* and *White Pelican Review.*

Marc Hofstadter, Walter Martin, Robert Sward, and Gary Young each read and critiqued the manuscript in earlier variations, for which the author extends his gratitude.

The author also wishes to thank Dorothy Ruef for digital assistance.

Cover artwork & design by Robert Weinstock.
Book design by Lisa Rappoport.

ISBN 978-1-930454-39-2

Direct all inquires to
Swan Scythe Press
1468 Mallard Way
Sunnyvale, CA 94087
http://www.swanscythe.com
Editor: Robert Pesich

Swan Scythe Press books are distributed by Small Press Distribution,
http://www.spdbooks.org

Printed in the United States of America.

for Carolyn Tipton

CONTENTS

Aging Heart

Some Teachers

Scratch Pegasus

The aging heart. To have loved and yet that nothing can be saved.
  —Albert Camus, *Notebooks*

Aging Heart

THRIFT SHOP

This dust has history, traces of closets
in whose deepest reaches lingered smells
of perfume that enveloped some smitten suitor
whose suits harbor evidence of a lovely arm
linked long since through his as they strolled the avenues
of a city that wouldn't stop, that persisted
in haunting them both all these years later.

The jacket now hangs in seedy light
amid the abandoned wardrobes of strangers
and knickknacks salvaged from living rooms
and the last uncracked plate of a set
that nobody bought at a yard sale
and various leftovers from love nests
settled here at the home for orphaned objects.

Warm fall weather just beyond the windows
evokes losses past, seasons whose subtle breezes
carried news of kitchens where dinner was cooking
as you bicycled by on the way home
or the breath of trees on some street you walked
alone late at night when you couldn't sleep
for the excitement of what you could sense coming.

It came and it went
and here's the evidence,
endless shelves stretching deathlessly,
knitting cities with this network of used suitcases
and scratched furniture where families
ate and sat, travelers packed their stuff,
old women read books and lovers slept entangled.

You're not looking for a life story
but things whisper and your own possessions
keep disappearing, so you find yourself
prowling these strange aisles where others
are all but present, their records a dollar each
and still playable on your turntable,
music of last nights longing for one more day.

ANTIQUITIES

The Etruscans enjoyed fucking,
according to these artifacts,

and the Greeks liked
fried squid on the beach,

and the Romans steaming plates
of pasta with red wine on the piazza.

At the senior living facility
where my mother is fading

into her last days, the ancient inmates
play games with the staff to stay entertained.

Strollers along the palisades on a cold day
at the solstice can see Point Dume easily

as gulls sail over the palms
and jets bank over the bay out of LAX.

It is all so old, almost eternal,
yet those aging through it are only temporary,

few of them even trying to leave a trace,
and the ones who do

doubting whether the tombs
they are carving so carefully

won't be erased for the value
of their real estate, or saved

for the sake of some museum
where a magnate slept

and kept a collection of looted art
to assuage what is inescapable.

BABS

She was a waitress at Delores's,
the drive-in at the corner of La Cienega
and Wilshire, where my father loved the chili
and they served those corkscrew french fries they called
Suzy Q's. She had dirty-blond hair and
little breasts and was about twenty-three
and her uniform fit her perfectly,
the light skirt softly hugging her slim hips,
and she had lovely legs, and a sweet smile.
A hamburger with ketchup, Suzy Q's
and a Coke were my idea of the perfect meal,
brought out on a tray by Babs with her graceful stride
on a Sunday night. I was in love with her.
She liked me too, but I was just four years old.

MEMORIAL DAY

Even between the spark arrestors
of the chimneys across the street
I can discern through the dusky haze
the outline of the smokestacks of the power plant
just above a faint blue slice of bay.
Waves of violence hammer the planet
and people walk their dogs in the gentle light,
which seems to forgive, absolve, all but erase.

The mockingbirds are talkative,
gossiping above rumors of tourists rumbling out of town
on Mission Street after a glorious day off,
and the smells of blooming lilies and magnolias
are mixed with herbicides and barbecue starter
as neighbors grill dinner and I sip my beer
thinking about the ones I never met
whose memories have been eradicated.

Mine too are temporary,
contingent on the whims
of those with whom I was entangled in time,
now living their evening reveries
in reinvented neighborhoods whose skies
are sliced by wires conducting
so many unintelligible messages
even the government couldn't catch them—

a chorus of complex intimacies,
confessions and incantations
only a drunken cantor might understand
in language even he knows is profane
and sacred at the same time,

a tongue unrecoverably corrupted
yet sweetened by birdsong at sundown
on a Monday at the end of May.

MAL DE TERRE

The land I stand on
    feels to be moving
away from beneath me
    ripping the roots
of the fruit trees I thought
    would keep dropping sweetness
onto my tongue
    forever but instead
are withering limb
    by bitter limb
as the climate turns
    and the ground drifts
under my sneakers
    and my jeans rip
and my lunch is unsettled
    by so many changes
I never expected
    the long days of summer
numbered anyway
    the moonlight fogged
my friends getting old
    and dropping dead
before we've finished
    our conversations
and those remaining
    are so annoying
I can hardly take
    another evening
stuck in their company
    that's why it seems
maybe it's me
    who's coming undone

from the dirt under me
       sickening into a dune
whose sand is rising
       slowly around my soul

IN THE BARKING PARK

In the barking park
where the city's dogs
socialize off leash sniffing each other's butts
and tangled strips of toilet paper
fly like flags from lampposts
and children run on summer's next-to-last day,
fat little finches hop and flit
to the rhythm of bicycle bells
and rusty ships float anchored on the river
like tired artifacts of industry
while sporty motorboats speed past celebrating the weekend
whose rain has blown inland
and whose wind shoves fall's first leaves along the paved walks
in a preview of the coming decline.
Mine is more plain,
the weight of what I bear
ever more evident with age
and its ailments I must not mention,
but you can imagine,
just multiply yours by the number of years
and subtract what's left,
a sum equal to the best pleasures
you can remember, thin but fine,
sweet as a girl's face
whose future is all in front
but also fragile, a long story
nobody knows, not even her weeping mom
who grieves with a strange gratitude
for what vanished before she understood what it was.
When someone records such things —
photographers, oral historians, those who wrote letters
in the old days before instantaneity
made everything ephemeral,

all those eccentric sentimentalists
who resisted writing their memoirs yet noted
what passed as it happened —
some trace almost remains,
less than a monument but slightly more
than a twig snapped twice
by the quiet wheels of a bike.

DEATH BY TIRAMISU

Throw me on top.
No, pull me up. No,
taste my grateful tears
as I take a bite of your lips.
This is the right way to die,
the heart caught by its tongue
in a kiss to arrest history

with fatal sweetness, with perfect
espresso- and rum-soaked richness
after a tender filet
consumed in a booth
in a room bathed in burgundy light,
facing a face whose beauty you've induced
endlessly in more rooms than you can remember,

in beds where you both were known to glow
with the immeasurable pleasure
of the familiar, increasingly unknown
as you deepen union
in speechless realms of redemption.
Thickly, the heart is happy
to stop with such satisfaction.

EURYDICE IS MISSING

Eurydice is missing. We were supposed to meet
in the lobby of the Underworld Hotel at cocktail hour
and adjourn to one of the lounges to weep over our breakup

but she didn't show. I asked at the desk if she'd left a message
and the clerk just looked at me with a strange expression,
but I'm not mad, just desperate to know what happened

after I stepped out of the elevator that night and turned
to find blank doors and the numbers above going down.
She was definitely difficult, a diva who hogged the spotlight

then complained about being stared at by strangers
who were only admiring her grace, her voice, the way she raised
her arms during her arias or moaned abandoned in my embrace.

We were going to have a drink and maybe take a room
but she disappeared and I don't have a clue where to.
So many loves have vanished and I never looked back,

maybe I missed them a little but not enough to follow them
into the depths again at the risk of everything, and anyway
this was something else, it was more like a vexing dream

where whatever I did to find her there was no connecting,
her willowy form lost among shadows in the deepening evening,
conventioneers with their badges gathering in the bars

laughing and hoping to score—all those hours in meetings
come down to this, a chance to get away to Hades
or whatever city this is, and be someone else relieved

of the wife and kids. But I am more desolate yet,
unable to reach Eurydice even on her cell,
the number rings and rings and no one answers.

CATHY M.

The gap between her front teeth turned me on
when I was a transfer student my junior year
at that bohemian college up on the Hudson.
She'd grown up in Greenwich Village and was cool
yet full of enthusiasm too, smart, warm and sweet,
with the best personality I'd ever met.
When we went to bed I didn't know what I was doing,
and in those promiscuous days she wasn't impressed
with my ineptitude. So she ended up
dumping me for another guy named Steve
who lived right down the hall from me in the dorm.
She married him and they moved to Santa Fe
where she opened a little cheese shop off the Plaza.
Then they divorced. She died of cancer at forty-four.

MARINA KOSHETZ

She lived next door to me in Malibu,
a Russian diva somewhat past her prime
who had been lovers with Rachmaninoff,
clearly the great passion of her life.
Now Archie Sparrow was her paramour,
an aging cowboy from New Mexico
whose back was banged up riding rodeo
and who played Hank Williams songs on his guitar.
They called themselves "The Sparrow and the Songbird"
and talked about writing a television series
or maybe a movie by that title, but
I doubt they ever got around to it.
Yet who could say their lives hadn't been rich,
busting broncs and fucking Rachmaninoff.

POEM IN OCTOBER

The mockingbird mimics a barking dog
and makes it sound sweet, nightingale-
like, as the Indian-summer sun
hits me in the chest with its heartwarming heat
and teenage girls in shorts ride by on bikes.

How can such an afternoon be allowed
to flash past without trying to fix it
in time, hold its momentous weight,
so mundane at the same time,
in some frame as a painter might,
tracing in spontaneous shapes on a flat plane
some slant of light unique that once,
and save it.

For what, a museum wall? A page
forgotten in some posthumous garage
where the grandchildren will rummage?

Even climate-controlled archives can't touch
such light as the composer tried to translate
into notes or the sky itself tried to reflect
to prove to its viewer his eyes weren't
deceiving themselves in the need
to see what's missing.

Just a love letter, really, words
arriving from afar over a signature
whose graceful strokes awaken those old desires
and evoke the touch of the hand that wrote.

THE SPANISH TILE TABLE

The Spanish tile table
is coming unglued in the sun
after decades shaded in the courtyard
of the house where my mother lived

for years with her backup man
after my dad was gone.
Now on the front deck of our bungalow,
a hazy blue peninsula in the distance,

the table is buckling under the glare
of a Mediterranean day,
my mother dead, her lover
gone long since,

the old man across the street
and me not far behind,
each of us more impermanent
than this work of an artisan.

Yet I can touch the table
and feel the painterly light,
its perfect warmth spilling
into my lap this afternoon.

A WEDDING POEM

for Claire & Alex

Fog is the first witness,
sneaking up early for a close look,

then the sun rolls in and beams on the scene,
then people—all these conspirators

surrounding and sealing the bonds
of the luckiest couple west of California.

They are off the charts,
transcending maps and weather.

It is beyond personal,
this intricate intimacy,

an improvisation, a composition
created in common in time

beginning long ago
and bringing into the future a certain

beauty, as in the healing of an imperfect
body, a design finding its form

to please the eye and gratify the heart.
Here is the shared art

of every day when dawn is doubly
revealed to be luminous

twice over in routine tenderness,
the touch of those who know

with whom they've awakened
and find themselves shining

in light that will last at least
two lifetimes.

6 June 2009

MAUDE'S POEM

What a babe you are in those old photographs,
such a voluptuous girl whose eyes are alive
to the promise of desire, dawn of a great romance
written in real time forever with your one man.

Sixty years later suddenly he was gone.

It threw my pitiful suffering into relief,
blue as I was mourning the loss of a muse.
Your calls, over all those miles, lifted me up
when you said my pages gave you more pleasure
than *The New Yorker* afforded, and I smiled
at the end of the line, alone in my kitchen
above the ocean, nursing an absence
I didn't know how to abandon,
grateful for such an impassioned ally.

We spoke of our respective solitudes,
yours so much more monumental than mine,
having lost the other with whom your entire
history was entwined; even the grandchildren
now were small consolation,
footnotes to a saga rooted in rhymed souls,
transcendent in its unending remembered
moments all but immortal.

Maude, you tough old broad,
even death couldn't quite take you down—
you died sitting up, like a poker player
raising the stakes on the strength
of your last Ace.

SKATEBOARD SONNET

A boy with a shaved head and a wiry girl,
black ponytail trailing, flash past the window
on this perfect May afternoon, Monterey
a purple outline across the bay, like the slope
of a thigh in profile, a reclining nude's
gift to the light in the spring sky, cut with streaks
of bird flight, overhead wires, car exhaust
and kids on skateboards powered by the grace
of their supple, muscular legs, sweet limbs later
to be entwined on a bed somewhere, at least
as I can see them through my own quick past.
It was on days like this, under such a sky,
my summer flowered without my knowing how
fleeting it was, like those kids who just whizzed by.

THE EUCALYPTS KEEP SEDUCING ME

The eucalypts keep seducing me
even as I glide with windows down in spring
under their overgrown galleries smelling deliciously medicinal,
their leaves glimmering silvery in the blue breeze.

It was a passing thing, this longing to be with trees
as with girls known ages since and seen today on the street,
spirals of desire pulling me downward into the years,
phantoms oblivious of their own allure.

Those gorgeous trees, those girls, my own
remembered possession, allow me to imagine
I'm still alive, still able to smell what can't be held,
to see what the breeze leaves.

DOTTY

I don't even remember how we met.
She was a fair-skinned, freckled strawberry blonde
who worked at the Bookshop, slender and shy
and a lot smarter than her silly name.
She had been married, and was just divorced.
When we first kissed, in the darkened newspaper
office downtown, after hours, on the way
to a poetry reading, her heart was beating
so hard I could feel it hammering through my jacket.
We spent one night together. Then she moved
back east, to Philly or New York, for art
school. Some years later I received a card
with a Romare Bearden jazz collage; inside,
she wrote: *This show reminded me of you.*

IN THE DARK

When wasn't it too late
to say what you meant
when you spoke in the dark.
Well not exactly spoke
but kind of groaned
your gratitude. If only
your interlocutor had
understood, and the page
you didn't even need
could have recorded
your undying oneness
with the one with whom
you are still inventing ways
to bewilder each other
deep in the strangest nights
you can remember, however
familiar they seem.
You are still blind
to her music, which
only means you hear it
more beautifully, and
find your eyes tasting
that face like a last meal:
this darkness nourishes
because it fills her absence
with delicious phantoms
you can almost touch.

FOREIGN FILMS

The haunted men in these movies
look nothing like me, resemble
myself only in their grieving
obsessive souls, their caught hearts

in memory's nets, in mysteries
of lost beauties whose faces
linger always in the photos
left on the sad shelves
and in the closed files,
the boxes of long-abandoned memorabilia.

These faces sometimes show up
as waitresses from some other film
whose dimples alone speak a language
demanding translation into new songs

of soloists who dine alone with smiles
on their minds across some table
where red wine tastes like Spain.

Where were those white teeth
in the sweet nights of Irish
or Argentinian cinema when
you walked out together into the teeming
streets to brush lightly against
the rushing multitudes, on the way
to your own unrated scene

with accents to match your crisply articulate
mouths whispering unspeakable endearments,
intimacies only the deepest midnight could witness,

or a leisurely afternoon
where you had nothing better to do
than lie down in the summer light
and find the hidden vein of all temporal
eternities, those flickering passions
that last forever, possessing
whoever had them.

THE LOVERS AT DEVIL'S SLIDE

Both in black jeans, black t-shirts,
sleek black car parked in the turnout,
he leaning back against the concrete barricade
at cliff's edge, precipitous drop
to the cold ocean below —
but the day is warm and clear
and she is pressing herself so hot
against him, kissing his mouth,
her slender curving body
seen in silhouette
as I breeze by on the highway—his eyes
glancing up to meet mine just in time
to glimpse my knowing grin —
and savor them diminishing in the mirror.

Some Teachers

My brother Rick is seventy today.
To me he'll always be about seventeen,
when I was nine and mimicked his every move
and whatever he did was suffused for me
with an aura of magic, mischief, grace and wit;
so I preferred to hang out with him and his friends
instead of kids my age, who were far less cool.
He wrote the funniest poems for his buddies,
modeled on classics from *The Golden Treasury*,
immortalizing the guys with witty rhymes.
Of course I started writing poems too,
trying to be as clever as he was, then
trying to please my friends, and later, girls.
But poetry was doing something to me.

He was my brother Bruce's closest friend,
the only child of Barbara Hutton, heiress
to the Woolworth millions, all those nickels
and dimes piled up into Lance's personal fortune.
He was handsome, blond, intelligent, and
my sister Mimi was in love with him.
He taught me how to play chess, and told me once,
You're not a kid, you're an evil little man.
He was a polo player and a racing driver;
he and Bruce drove fast cars and had hot girls.
Lance married Jill St. John; then they divorced.
Later he married Cheryl the Mouseketeer.
At thirty-six, flying his plane one night
over Colorado, he crashed into a mountain.

WILLIAM WILSON

He worked for us when I was a little kid;
he did the heavy stuff around the house,
fixing this and that, cooking sometimes,
driving Grandma where she needed to go
and hanging out with me when he had the time.
My folks were working long hours at the office
and traveling a lot, so I was left
to fend for myself or tag along with William.
Women would call sometimes and ask for him.
He had a long scar on his knee from a grenade
in World War II, had played semipro ball
and driven semi trucks all over the country.
I revered him. Later my father learned
he had a criminal record a mile long.

DAVE BLAKEMORE

He was the toughest coach I ever had,
a lanky thinker who understood the game's
most subtle nuances and strategies,
a baseball savant whose skeletal physique
earned him the nickname "Bones." Like a Zen priest
he taught the fine art of paying attention,
being attuned to what was happening,
responding in the moment with precision.
*Make the ground ball go through, don't get doubled
on a line drive,* I can still hear him shout
from the coach's box when I was in scoring position,
which meant know where the ball is before you run.
Later he made a fortune in real estate.
He advised my brother to move every five years.

Señor Padilla was short, with a bald head
and a big potbelly that bulged over his belt.
His name was Juan and he was Mexican
but he spoke English with no discernible accent;
his colleagues, I learned later, called him Johnny
in the faculty lounge at Beverly Hills High.
I took his Spanish 1A as a freshman
beginning to learn vocabulary and grammar
under his instruction, which was patient,
direct and brilliant, easily understood,
and I stayed in his classes through all four years.
His favorite poet was Bécquer; he would recite
those beautiful lines and almost swoon with pleasure.
I owe him more than I can ever repay.

JESÚS CHAVARRÍA

He was my high school American history teacher,
a handsome young man with a pockmarked face,
black hair and the faintest trace of a Mexican accent.
He showed up the first day of class in my junior year,
surveyed the room full of restless adolescents
and launched into a speech something like this:
Ever since the beginning of time, man
has had to overcome temptations, obstacles
to achievement and the ordeals of hunger,
thirst and the labor of earning a living.
The burdens of civilization can be heavy,
the sacrifices great, the path to success
steep, but discipline is rewarded.
So, there will be no talking in this class.

MISS MASACAS

Usted pronuncia bastante bien,
she said to me once when I'd read aloud in class.
She was from Argentina, with that accent
that liquefies the double Ls and rolls
the Y sound into a fluid rush between
the teeth, the tongue softly withheld—though I
was just eighteen and barely knew how to kiss.
Miss Masacas had come from Buenos Aires
to teach Spanish at UCLA, and I
was lucky enough to be a freshman, probably
aced the course, but what I remember is
how beautiful she was, blonde with olive skin
and a kind smile, and how sitting atop her desk
she liked to show off her extraordinary legs.

HANS MEYERHOFF

He taught philosophy at UCLA
when I was a freshman, just beginning to read.
On the stage of the lecture hall in Haines
he would pace from one side to the other,
uncut gray fringe ringing his bald dome
which shone in the dim academic light.
He spoke of Plato and the Dialogues,
and did his imitation of Socrates,
not so much with his questions—there were hundreds
of us—but by the simple act of being
a real philosopher, still questioning
ideas, existence, ethics, understanding.
One morning early in the next semester, he
was killed in a head-on crash on Sunset Boulevard.

He seemed a little depressed a lot of the time
teaching the Shakespeare seminar at Bard,
and when he spoke those lines of Lear declaring
"As flies to wanton boys are we to the gods—
they kill us for their sport," the bitterness
in his voice is something I can hear
still, more than forty years later. He was an actor,
of course, and taught theater too, so who knows what
was moving inside him to make him sound like that.
I wasn't planning an academic career
and he found that refreshing, but I *could write
anyway*, he told me, *write professionally.*
So this week I belatedly called to thank him.
He sounded old, not well, but said, *Keep going.*

He had such a beautiful Castilian accent
and his voice was beautiful, too—he was an actor
in his spare time when he wasn't teaching Cervantes
or the poets of the Golden Age, or translating
Alberti's memoirs. He was the only professor
I made friends with when I was in graduate school;
maybe it was his beauty, dark and lean,
with that little goatee—he looked like a Spaniard,
though he was a Jew from New York City. We
just had some kind of natural connection.
Now his wife calls to tell me he's dead, and
all I can remember is his question the night
I read my Cernuda translations at City Lights:
How did you get it to sound so much like Spanish?

Wild Men

SONNY ROLLINS AT ZELLERBACH

The man is big but bent over
    and sort of lurches, hobbling,
        toward center stage,
loud red tunic hanging loose on his huge frame,
    wild white hair, an Albert Einstein Afro,
        big Mosaic beard,
horn in his mouth,
    and soon an astonishing sound
        soars in the hall
as the rhythm section—
    guitar, electric bass, drums and percussion—
        kicks into a tight groove
and the music heats up fast, cooking,
    quickly brought to a boil
        as he rocks and nods
through the first song,
    each player rhythmically finding his fit
        in the bigger sound
driven by the gold sax of the master
    now pushing eighty and pumping out the power
        of all those years
through seasoned lungs, joyfully, just breathing,
    it seems, driving high air through the horn
        and tickling its keys
so the valves breathe just so
    and the reed sings
        brightly through the bell,
which segues into a sentimental ballad,
    lifted so far beyond its origins
        it's scarcely the same song and yet a true
translation, evincing the latent soul
    in a tired tune, transformative
        power of the artist expertly displayed

in the course of his routine task,
      inventing in the present
         a fresh exaltation
of existence emerging in the moment
      out of a lost past, now shifting
         into a homegrown calypso,
rhythm gearing up into a driving groove,
      guitar in a sweet drone underpinning the horn's
         sharp riffs, irresistible rhythms
the legs and feet can't help moving along with,
      head nodding, bopping in place, an amazed grin
         on the face, what art is for,
to move you, to raise the stakes
      transfusing the ordinary night
         with unrepeatable beauty, one-time-only
joy as the notes and the syncopation
      hypnotize the hall
         and a thousand witnesses feel
what sweetens the spirit through dark days,
      giving the tired soul strength to return
         tomorrow to the mundane,
but this is beyond, way outside,
      a wild wonder corralled
         in a five-part blend
of crafty fabrication on the spot,
      improvising relief and resurrection,
         the streaming enlightenment of revelation.

When Edgar met Audrey
at a Red Death benefit
and they were soon dating
and were seen at Elaine's
or Ciro's or Ruth's Chris
Steakhouse in San Francisco,
jetting from one enchanted
city to another in a frenzy
of fresh romance, the gossip
columnists were beside themselves
speculating on the couple's
spectacular sex life,
Hepburn's delicate elegance
and Poe's drunken abandon
inflaming the imaginations
of the magazines, their pictures
appearing everywhere, often
in flight from paparazzi
yet dignified always
and resigned to tolerating
their strange fame, now
compounded by their alliance.
Those were times when a
writer's lines were remembered
and a star's face blazed
with beauty only a poet
could begin to perceive
and celebrate in its true
subtlety, inventing rhymes
to imitate the symmetry
of cheekbones and deep
brown eyes, balladworthy
tragic features doomed

like his to an early demise.
Watching their films
on my flat-screen plasma
home entertainment system
on these perfectly restored
director's-cut DVDs, replete
with exclusive interviews
and outtakes where the stars'
affection is obvious, I sip
my absinthe and honor
their integrity, vulnerable
to every terrible public
humiliation yet poised
as they were taken down
by the burden of their renown.
Audrey, Edgar, your genius
shines, your unlikely love
a tale I'll relate to anyone
still listening at this late
hour when so few know you
anymore truly as you were.

ODYSSEUS IN A BAR IN ITHACA

The couple has resumed
the routine of marriage
while he keeps humming
in his wandering head
a calypso he heard
at sea that he can't forget.
Home is normal now,
a gift to be lived in,
but what he remembers
torments him because
he felt so alive
in his suffering.
He goes out for a drink
one night by himself,
thinking about his age,
how immortality grows
on him, even as darkness
bears down with new doom.
These late December days
in the old hometown
have in them traces
of the unspeakable,
even though something
begs to be spoken
or sung, like the songs
crooned in this dive
by a singer too drunk
on hard luck to know
how soulful she is.

DON'T LET THEM GIVE YOU THAT LOBOTOMY

Don't let them give you that lobotomy.
Those pills are just an ice pick by another name.
Better to be a madman than a zombie.

And what is madness? To recognize your mother
for what she is? See your own family,
like everyone's, as a disaster? Imagine yourself
guilty of poetry, perpetrator of gratuitous music?

Better to choose your own poison than have some sham
shaman prescribe what the pharmacists have sold him.

You are not crazy, you are responding
with natural anguish to destiny's jokes—
the house, the car, the kids, the career,
sirens crying across incomprehensible landscapes, time
taking what you never had but thought was yours

and now the truth is more naked than you knew
and nothing helps. This is the way it is, too bad,
and we must play ball, deal, be cool
as we call a spade a spade, a soul a soul.

Don't let the doctors drive their stainless steel
into the sharpest part of your brain.

Relish your lost mind and embrace the mania,
just keep it contained, and when the spirit hits,
write. You are a poet.

MY BEST FRIEND

He had a deadly tumor removed from his head
and the wound patched up with skin from his left thigh,
which as a side effect gave him a new face.

_____

He moved too fast and snapped his Achilles tendon
while playing tennis with his ten-year-old
and hopped around on crutches for six months.

_____

When the sutures from her open-heart surgery tore,
he saved his eighty-year-old mother-in-law's life,
expertly closing the wound with a butterfly bandage.

_____

He wrote for his creative writing students
more than a hundred letters of recommendation,
thereby neglecting to write a hundred poems.

_____

His ancient Volvo was making a funny sound
one morning, so he looked under the hood
and found a wood rat staring back at him.

_____

The doctor detected a tumor on his testicle,
so he let them cut him open to have it removed,
and it turned out not to be a tumor after all.

———————————

He came within a hair of losing his job
when his boss asked what he thought of the new hire
and he told her, without thinking, what he thought.

———————————

When everything in his life was tormenting him,
he cooked Thanksgiving dinner for twenty people
to take his mind off what was tormenting him.

———————————

He drove five hundred miles in blinding rain
in the dark to visit his father on Christmas Eve
and when he arrived the old man wasn't home.

———————————

His mechanic didn't even give him a discount
when his Volvo set what seemed like a world record
for consecutive nervous breakdowns in one year.

———————————

He and his wife threw an after-Christmas party
to take their minds off the fact they were so broke
they couldn't even afford to throw a party.

———————————

He won the Job Award at his synagogue
for most consecutive months of suffering,
the first non-Jew ever to receive that honor.

———————————

He wondered aloud how it could ever have been
that all we seemed to do when we were young
was read, write poetry, smoke pot and fuck.

———————————

We smoked marijuana together for twenty years,
gazing out over the Boardwalk and the bay
and saying, *It doesn't get any better than this.*

To explain the life of a man is no easy task,
you wrote all those years ago, and it's true,
but lots of painters have made a good try, you added.
You also said that poets are born to lose,
and lose big, and you can say that again.
You gave it all away ahead of time,
getting the jump on loss, taking a chance
on tapping out a few lines at a time
for no good reason, just to set down whatever
was delivered to go along with the drinks
and the cigarettes. You've made your getaway,
Greg, like the thief you were—beneath the law,
below good and evil, under the radar,
stealthily erasing your caper in real time.

MUSTAFA

He stopped me on the street in Casablanca
and asked me if I'd like to smoke some hash.
Something about his shades was sinister.
I nodded coolly, yes, of course I would.
We started walking, walked all over the city
most of the afternoon, stopping in cafés
to smoke hashish-laced cigarettes and drink
mint tea. After more than a week at sea
it felt good to be high. I was energized
even though he was trying to wear me out.
He said we were going to his sister's house
for couscous, and to give him all my money
so we could buy a gift for her. Yeah, sure.
I gave him a twenty just to get rid of him.

WILD MAN

I didn't wish to be civilized
but the time came.
They took me from my cave
by way of a woman, and I left
my weapons, my collection of
hi-fi mating calls and the wall
where I painted in my own blood
pictures of what I hunted.
Gathering a few hides
for the long drive to the suburbs
I said goodbye to the sweet monsters
of my solitude and learned to walk
the streets on a leash and sniff
the breeze for signs of secret
wildness. Beasts like me
can survive in this Edenless
outpost because we keep close
to the vest our explosive love,
the high desire no advertising
can touch, which binds souls
and provokes contradiction
among critics who see
in such controlled passion
their own absent obsessions.
I came down but could not help
painting in blood.
The hunt continues.

THE COLONEL'S GARDEN

The colonel's garden runs all the way down to the river,
and his house, which he designed and built by hand,
has an upstairs terrace where he can drink beer
and watch the sun go down behind the trees
and try to forget his years with the secret police.

HOUSEGUEST IN A GATED NEIGHBORHOOD

The guard in the gatehouse
has gone home for the night
and I am locked outside.

Any burglar could climb the fence
but why, when what's in there
is just more stuff,

nothing to bother stealing.
Even the conversations
gently echoing in memory

are just lost sounds and lovely
faces in the mind,
the line between this and that

a slow blur where what was
for a minute or few is no more.
Now cool light covers the hills

and a blossomy breeze caresses my black shirt
and cars curl uphill and down over Decker Canyon
to the sound of sprinklers where only

decades ago and last night desert dogs
loped hopelessly across acres of scrub
and dust—prickly,

you might call the brush
hugging the slopes, scratchy
if you touched it,

but who could from here.
The gate is locked,
the guard is gone,

my car parked outside, lights
on, engine a hum, no place
else to go and no cellphone.

A CLOSE READING OF GENIUS

Did I read this book
or did it read me—

the wicked lines of my friend & rival's verse
slap me upside the psyche like his acclaim,
        those prizes he collects
and tosses in back of his closet like lost socks.

He can dig the vanity of winning,
takes the pose of a tough guy,
the Bogart of poetry—
        just too sensitive
almost for words—
        but no Bacall;
the last one fled with his fellowship.

So he records what escapes him,
        and in turn us,
with gritty twists and surprise
        non sequiturs
that keep circling back to tag up.

Am I inspired, or bemused?
Flummoxed, or befuddled?
Excited, or violated?
Exasperated, or infused
with a weird grandeur?

His eclectic erudition is winsome,
like a roomful of Afghan schoolgirls.

I wish I had half
his alcohol content,
proof of ruthless truths
told offhandedly, like jokes
of an old Jew in a saloon after shul.

This God of yours is not credible,
leaving those piles of shoes,
           those spectacles.

I can scarcely discern the outline
of a skyline, the rooftops are too
spangled with escapists
gazing at the stars.

These are the days our grandmothers bored us about,
recounting their sicknesses,
their surgeries.
Suddenly aged, we touch the remote
and find the same jive on five hundred channels.

If only I could writhe like a charmed snake
rising to the sound of a Monk solo,
or fish my share of sunken loves out of the old reservoir,
or crash my Porsche for immortality's sake,
I might know what to make of my man's masterpiece—
           but I can't. I am a flawed witness

to brilliance, shielding my eyes
from the glare off his shades.

DRIVING A STAKE THROUGH THE HEART OF BEATNIK VAMPIRES

Out of the bars of North Beach
Out of the backseats of '55 Chevys
Out of ducked-down alleyways six blocks from Venice Beach
Out of the seedy cafés of Greenwich Village
and the soulfully seedier dives of Negro neighborhoods
where whitemen go to try to get down and funky

From Tibetan mountaintops and Moroccan casbahs
From highway truck stops and Buddhist temples
From spiritual quests and boozy binges
From smoke-filled pads where the joint is passed perpetually
From groovy coffeehouses where they howl to the beat of bongos
From bandstands where they try to keep up with the jazzmen
Out of drunken macho weepy tough-guy sentimentality
Out of hours huddled over notebooks composing incantatory odes

The undead beatniks come

Dragging their cigarette butts and their sorry asses
Wearing their unshaved mugs and their soggy berets
Their fishnet-leggy babes in their black turtlenecks
inexplicably hanging onto their arms
Popping their pills, puffing their smokes, desperately chugging their beers
and claiming to speak for all the beat-down souls
and all the beatific hard-luck angel food cake eaters

From the stages of poetry festivals and political demonstrations
The undead Beats keep coming unstoppably
Hijacking open mikes and polite salons
With their canned rebellion long past its sell-by date
With their wine-stained teeth and their raggedy manuscripts
With the cool idea that poetry corrupts the young
and that verses rhymes with versus and they are against Everything

They must be stopped and sent back to the last century
We must redeem our silver crosses from the pawnshops
and our bespoke suits from the haberdashers
We must empty all the old ashtrays and fire up the dishwashers
We must wash the hair of the bedraggled and clip their toenails
We must teach them to read Tennyson again
and Longfellow and Kipling and Eliot and Strunk & White
We must send them back to get their MFAs
We must feed them fast food to slow down their meth metabolism

They must be stopped because if they continue to come
They will drag the sixties behind them, what a nightmare

Never again

Never again the speed-rapping metaphysical inanities
Never again the crab lice
Never again that all-night taste in the mouth
Wrong kisses on the tongue wrong juices on the upholstery
Never again the self-righteous self-pitying rambling rants and snivelings
Never again the whining over spilled wine

The beatnik vampires must be stopped or they will suck us dry
They will drag us into the swamps of their arrested adolescence
They will pull us down into the depths of their dusty couches
where we will succumb to their bohemian sitcoms
They will drive us again forever down dead-end roads
They will wrap their speeding Oldsmobiles around trees
and us without seatbelts in the shotgun seat
They will run red lights and blue lights in pursuit of what can't be caught
and in the process crash our careers as creative writers

We must stop them
We must resolve to resist their market research
We must rip their commodified khakis off their behinds
We must unsubscribe from their spam
We must delete their apps from our iPhones
We must purge their works from our Kindles
and offload their archives from our iPads
We must smash their icons and hijack their typewriters
We must repossess their beat-up broken-down Buicks
We must drive our skateboards and our redwood stakes
into their undead hearts

Scratch Pegasus

JOURNEY IN A BRUSHSTROKE

He couldn't work because the ink was frozen
so he had to wait for spring to release the river
on which he would launch his fragile imagined boat

the long interlude is syncopated
by the sound of an elevator
moving slowly between museum floors

where galleries open into ancient landscapes
and cultures so remote you can smell their silences
reach up through layers of lost ages

asking to be remembered by anyone
however distracted by their own fading civilizations
professional problems familial obligations

so distant from these whispering scrolls
mountains and streams to which the old recluses
fled from the corruptions of their governments

POEM I CAN'T DECIPHER INSCRIBED ON A STONE

Tiny red characters intricately carved
above the Chinese sage in robes
whose eyebrows have grown so long
he appears to be braiding them
seem to be telling me feel
in your hand the weight
of this smooth stone quarried
from an ancient mountain
cut into small irregular shapes
polished and carved to stand
on some distant desk or shelf
to speak in sweet ambiguities
swirls of darkness moving
through fields of daylight caught
in landscapes concise enough
to fill your palm and be
held in your ignorant fingers

SILENCING THE WRITINGS

for Richard O. Moore

Where there is no I
the eye sees more
or less clearly, says
what it knows it
can't know

really, and yet
what it does is
to search, to seek
out those few
words that touch

what is real.
What is sung, even
spoken, philosophically
speaking, is that
what can be called

real? Or is the lost
knowledge only that
which can't be
touched, and thus
followed, longingly,

infinitely

———————————

Not so fast, wise
guy, just because
lines on a white
page with stripes
line up like some

kind of logic
doesn't mean they
mean what they
seem to say,
they more like point

away from what
is there to know
because what is
certain anyway,
anywhere out there

where thought stops
and things in them-
selves appear
beyond our seeing
or saying them?

———————————

We reach—you and
whoever it is tran-
scribing this—past
points of no re-
turn or reference

toward what we (I
and whoever else)
don't quite grasp
just past what passes
understanding, an

apprehension of wit-
nessing something,
some naked woman,
let's say, or wild
animal that ran

once across a road
or lay on a bed
in memory as we
embodied being or
swore we saw some-

thing wholly alive,
a kind of proof
or illusion of
persuasion, true
enough anyway

to stay still, held
inside a head so
full of itself it
hardly knows what
to make of its own

thinking

WHAT DID YOU LOSE

What did you lose that you never wrote—
only the music moving through your heart
when no need moved you to record its notes.

LIGHT STREAMS

Gold light streams
through cold beer

on a June afternoon
in a city strolled

by men in suits
after work or in short-

sleeved shirts clutching
little cameras or devices

connecting them elsewhere
while right here streams

of lovely girls strut
proudly along streets

to meet their beaus
for a drink or simply be

in the streaming moment,
streaks of the unkeepable,

the kind that keep you
grateful for every trace

of grace granted the stray
hours outside time, eternally

temporary and all the more
keenly perceived, piercing

the perceiver like one of those
blades Borges romanticized

in Buenos Aires
a century since,

still sharp, still
vital and fatal.

FLAMENCO NIGHT AT LULU'S CAFÉ & JUICE BAR

I used to be bohemian
but now I'm Andalusian
listening to tall heels
hammer the bandstand
on Saturday night
in Sacramento, sipping
a pint of Sierra Nevada
as if Granada were
just outside instead
of my home state
stolen from Spain
for its snow and gold.
The singer resembles
one of my ex-loves
whose bed in Bodega Bay
consoled me for some
few months of grief
relieved by her sweet
body even though it
wasn't hers I had
lost, and the birds'
cries were benevolent
through the fog of dawn.
Under her black hat
she could almost pass
for a Spaniard, and
her black-haired
partner with the
lace sleeves and long
scarf and silver ear-
rings has the moves
of a mourner trans-
formed by sunlight

and dark guitars
into flames of her
own making, flying
into the mild night
with fierce grace
and wild quick light.

MIDNIGHT SIDEWALKS

I like it when the waitresses change clothes.
At the end of the shift they shed their uniforms
and step out looking like civilians newly alive,
springing up the street away from the restaurant
to meet their lovers or a group of girlfriends
with whom they'll sit for a drink in some bar
or café where they can laugh at leisure
while other young men or women serve them before
their turn to escape and move the cycle around —
these endless circles whose rhythmic movements
are mimicked by hips in rotating motion
in black slacks along the city's sidewalks
to the endless gratitude of thirsty eyes
with nothing to do but watch what passes
from the cheap seats after a bargain meal
served under an umbrella by a bald waiter
on a street behind the cathedral in Seville.

EPIPHANY ON WEST 44TH STREET

Walking down the street without their instruments
musicians look like almost anyone else—

just as the air appears to the eye transparent
despite the scent of, say, honeysuckle
in some small-town alleyway of an April evening.

Why, when so little is left to be said,
must virtuosos hammer their keyboards
until some harmony is manifest,

some name pronounced that suggests
a timeless face unseen since the Renaissance
when its features were first invented

only to be repeated in perpetuity
on every street where eyes are engaged
in recording what is constantly being lost,

those traces of the eternal that remain.

LEE MORGAN WAS HERE

The horns onstage
summon sounds so old
they resurrect lost lips

and lungs, hearts so broke
they explode with emotion
turned to lusty technique

blowing impassioned notes
through countless years' scores,
those wide pages spread

with fluttering black spots
over straight lines where bird-
like marks can be read

by virtuoso decoders
channeling dark spirits,
bright flickerings of the city's

soul, those hard edges with curves
of urbane women, taxicab horns
and long circular exhalations of ecstasy

PARKING GARAGE

Note how the fumes
don't quite kill you,
and the fenders gleam in the dull
fluorescent glow.
That little ticket spit from the machine
is something like a tongue
speaking an exotic idiom.
And when the gate goes up
letting you in or out
you are crossing into the underworld
or into the everyday myth
of the vivid city.

Rilke's attempt to read on a gloomy afternoon
in a coffee shop in Seattle proves impossible
due to the pop songs piped through the ceiling
and the TV talk show with slithering headlines and
subtitles crawling across the bottom of the screen,
all the noise needed to distract anyone
from the quietude of the fine drizzle outside,
so meditative amid the rush-hour agitation.

Lou Andreas-Salomé is sipping a latte
and scribbling a memoir, but Rainer Maria
feels ill at ease amid the red décor
and patrons tapping at their laptops.
He'd prefer a private office in the highrise upstairs
where he might look down at the traffic and from there
see spirits streaming through the streets,
those streaks of taillights leaving their signatures
which signify individuals
shuttling between one oblivion and another
with their unanswerable questions, their mundane
riddles and ridiculously poignant
practical and philosophical problems.

Why for example exist only to vanish
leaving no evidence beyond a few boxloads
of garage-sale stuff destined for the dump
once the estate has been liquidated?
Whose rose fades faster and lets fall its eyelids,
the unhomed one who's lost his family
smoking absently ambling down the concrete
or the librarian on the way back from a break
walking briskly along the wet sidewalk without a hat?

Whose cappuccino steams watching the plate glass weep?
Whose grammar fails in the face of the unsayable?

From Vincent's hospital window, a walled
wheatfield—the same one trembling with color
in the other pictures—appears to be suffering
yet also thriving under sheets of driving rain,
the canvas behind the sheet of non-glare glass
stopping me as I walk,
still dazed by a small Cézanne,
through this wing of the museum in late October.
The Giants are playing the Phillies tonight in the playoffs
and every bar in town will be tuned to that green Eden
of grown men behaving like boys on a summer day.
Vincent's picture is almost grim, so gray and muted
through the downpour, but look closely
into the slanting streaks
and hundreds of colors ravish your seized eyes,
like all those lovely faces you'll never touch,
and so his terrible sadness touches you, drenches you
like the expansive landscape under that storm of emotion
the painter caught and drove through the strokes of his brushes.
After an hour I'm saturated and must exit
past the construction, down the long broad steps
and back downtown along Benjamin Franklin Parkway,
returning to the world of hotels and homelessness
and games through which we escape for a while
into the timeless grace of double plays, impossible catches
and pitchers who look too young to throw such tricky strikes.
How strange that Vincent's tears will outlast the winners' fame.

Picasso's electrician, seventy-one years old,
has revealed his cache of the master's paintings,
notebooks, drawings, miscellaneous items
given in exchange for service
keeping the lights on in the late years.
How many hundreds of millions they will fetch
is anyone's guess, but first the family will fight
to prove old Pablo never would have
so cavalierly spread his treasure to a handyman.
Yet why not, with so much excess creation to spare,
hand some over to the help: a paycheck
that pays in kind, my work for yours, a fair exchange,
true economics of art, more rich than cash.
I like the sound of it: "Picasso's electrician."

HOPPER

Hopper's representation,
so square compared to his successors' transgressions,
looks now purely formal and coolly classical
while so much subsequent experiment

is revealed as inconsequential,
conceptual gimmicks for critics to figure out
and philosophize about for the sake of discourse,
to which art is subordinate.

Hopper endures
as one who held true to his vision
while the hipsters pursued the new,
the old fart stroking the forms

into planes of shimmering light
that stays fresh through ages of cliché,
the familiar images
plastered on posters and calendars

unable to exhaust the actual pictures
exposed in their unique strangeness on plain walls
in rooms full of murmuring tourists
relieved to see what they recognize.

I find myself surprised
by what I thought I knew,
amazed by the newness of the abused,
the artist's truth transcending his success.

The tulip magnolia is spouting its little flames
and the pyracantha in the backyard is hot
with those bright-red blood-beads like police-car lights
and one lone calla lily flutes its white face toward the sky
out of a rain-glazed palette of shiny green
this Sunday afternoon before the solstice.

My wife—how strange it remains to say those words—
is out for a walk before it gets dark
but may linger to watch the Christmas lights come on,
and to keep my fingers occupied I'm typing
a few lines impressed on this tired ribbon
before performing an upgrade on the Olivetti.

I notice by the number on the clock radio I'm missing the news
but the green tinge of its digits is such a perfect shade
of stoplight brightness that I hesitate to hit the button
so it can compete with the sound of kids on skateboards
scraping by outside. This morning it sounded like a bird
might be caught in the chimney, I couldn't be sure

whether its trills and whistles were distress signals
or just the cheerful announcement of its pleasure
in the brisk weather as it paused in its rounds
on our spark arrestor. What is it about time
that gets the old poets going here at the brink
of winter when the days break off

like crumbling bluff edges and the nights
grow increasingly cold, and flannel is a comfort.
The bird, which looked dovelike but I don't think was
a dove because it was much too lyrical, flew off
when I opened the door to determine whether I had to call
some rescue squad to save us from its song.

SCRATCH PEGASUS

Scratch Pegasus. Last week in a workout
the exercise boy—a girl from the North Bay
who dropped out of school to ride poetry—
heard under the colt's hoofbeats

a rhythm that didn't scan, that seemed
to lift off the track at odd intervals
and soar into the morning light
for long caesuras

between hitting the turf with a rumbling report
that seemed to sound for its own sake instead of speed—
the horse, she said, was spooked
but in a way she'd never felt before

under her boots, under her floating
butt in the saddle which had the feeling
of flying just as the sun was climbing
the sky behind the backstretch and the scent

of roses out of nowhere
knocked her off center and she fell,
but the horse kept rising—
now she could see him sailing above the stables

as his trainer dropped the stopwatch
and drew his cellphone to dial 911
while the beautiful animal cleared the hills
and banked downtown as if drawn by the smell

of dusty books in some secondhand store
where unpublished poets browse in hopeful despair,
looking for lines that will take flight
out of an otherwise ordinary page

and singe their lips with the grace of revelation
that transcends speed or any race
to succeed. Scratch Pegasus.
He wins by disappearing into the sky.

STEPHEN KESSLER is the author of eight previous books and chapbooks of original poetry, fifteen books of literary translation, two collections of essays, *Moving Targets* and *The Tolstoy of the Zulus*, and a novel, *The Mental Traveler*. He was a founding editor of the independent literary publishers Green Horse Press and Alcatraz Editions, the international journal *Alcatraz*, and the newsweeklies the *Santa Cruz Express* and *The Sun*. Since 1999 he has edited the award-winning literary newspaper *The Redwood Coast Review*. He is also the editor and principal translator of *The Sonnets* by Jorge Luis Borges. His translations of Luis Cernuda, *Written in Water* and *Desolation of the Chimera*, have received a Lambda Literary Award and the Harold Morton Landon Translation Award from the Academy of American Poets, respectively. For more about Stephen Kessler, visit www.stephenkessler.com.

Scratch Pegasus was printed at Community Printers in Santa Cruz, California, on 80lb. Finch vanilla vellum paper, with 80lb. Sterling matte covers. The typeface is Monotype Van Dijck, based on a font designed by Christoffel Van Dijck in Amsterdam in the 1660s. The titling is Paul Renner's Futura.